I CAN DO HARD THINGS

My Journey Toward Reconciliation, Recovery, and Healing

Laura Pardo

ISBN 979-8-88851-784-0 (Paperback)
ISBN 979-8-88851-785-7 (Digital)

Covenant Books
11661 Hwy 707
Murrells Inlet, SC 29576
www.covenantbooks.com

To my dad, for his selfless gift of time and love during this journey—an extension of his servant heart and love for Christ that he bestowed on me throughout my life. Thank you, Dad, for always making me feel like your little girl.

For Chuck, in loving memory of a life too short. We will meet again on the golden streets; in the meantime, rest pain-free in the arms of Jesus.

INTRODUCTION

*You can't go back and change the beginning, but you
can start where you are and change the ending.*
— C. S. Lewis

If you are like me, you probably do not think much about your blood, what it does for your health, and what happens if it is diseased. I learned much about my blood when I was diagnosed with amyloidosis, a rare blood disorder.

As I recount my health journey, from mysterious symptoms to a stem cell transplant, it seems necessary to understand blood cells, bone marrow, and stem cells.[1]

What is bone marrow?

Bone marrow is a spongy material in large bones like the femur (thigh), hip, and ribs. Bone marrow is made up of cells called hematopoietic stem cells. Hematopoietic cells are transplanted to the patient during a stem cell transplant.

Hematopoietic stem cells are *baby* cells that become white blood cells, red blood cells, or platelets. They grow and are stored in the bone marrow until they are needed. Each type of cell has a job:

- white blood cells (leukocytes): cells that help fight infection

---

[1] This following information comes from OncoLink at the University of Pennsylvania.

- red blood cells (erythrocytes): cells that carry oxygen from the lungs to the rest of the body and return carbon dioxide to the lungs as waste
- platelets (thrombocytes): cells that help the body form blood clots to control bleeding

What does autologous mean?

Autologous means that the transplanted cells come from the patient's own body. Many people think a transplant must be something taken from a donor (another person), but that would be called an allogeneic transplant. In an autologous transplant, the patient *donates* their cells to themselves. I had an autologous stem cell transplant.

How do we collect these cells?

When providers first started doing stem cell transplants, the only way to get stem cells was directly from the bone marrow. This is where the term *bone marrow transplant* comes from. In the past, the cells would be collected in the operating room by inserting needles into the patient's hip bones to remove the bone marrow. Stem cells were removed from the marrow, preserved in dimethyl sulfoxide (DMSO), and frozen until needed.

In recent years, providers found that giving a medication called granulocyte colony-stimulating factor, or GCSF, stimulates the stem cells to be released from the bone marrow and into the bloodstream. Using a blood test, they can tell how many cells are in the bloodstream. Once the number is high enough, the cells are removed from the patient through a process called apheresis[2]. With apheresis, there is no longer a need to remove stem cells from bone marrow in an operating room.

---

[2] Apheresis is the removal of blood plasma from the body by the withdrawal of blood, its separation into plasma and cells, and the reintroduction of the cells, used especially to remove antibodies in treating autoimmune diseases.

Here's the process for harvesting stem cells:

- Stem cells are removed using a catheter/port inserted into the chest wall.
- Blood is taken out, run through the apheresis machine to remove the stem cells, and the rest of the blood is returned to the patient.
- The cells are frozen in the same DMSO preservative that is used for bone marrow. Preserving the cells on ice, called cryopreservation, is needed because the cells must be harvested a few weeks before the actual transplant.

What is meant by transplant?

To understand stem cell transplants, one needs to know about chemotherapy. Chemotherapy is a group of medications that work by killing rapidly dividing cells in the body. Cancer cells (and amyloids[3]) tend to divide and spread quickly. With an autologous transplant, providers give the patient high doses of chemotherapy to wipe out the bone marrow but then *rescue* the bone marrow using the patient's stem cells (collected earlier, before chemotherapy).

How is the transplant done?

The patient receives high doses of chemotherapy to try to kill any cancer cells/amyloids in the body. The patient will then rest for one or two days to let the body process and clear out the chemotherapy so that the new cells are not damaged.

On the day of the transplant, the patient is given medications to prevent any reactions to the DMSO preservative and intravenous (IV) fluids. Blood pressure and heart rate are closely watched, and the frozen stem cells are thawed. They are returned to the patient like a blood transfusion through an intravenous line.

---

[3]   Rogue cells that form the basis of my disease.

After infusing the stem cells, where do they go?

The transplanted stem cells find their way back to the bone marrow space and get to work. When the stem cells arrive in the bone marrow, things are in bad shape—almost all the old marrow cells have been killed by the chemo. The stem cells start making new white and red blood cells and platelets. It can take anywhere from seven to fourteen days for the stem cells to make new cells and for those new cells to mature enough to work the way they should.

What happens after the transplant?

This waiting period is often the hardest part. Blood cell counts are very low, putting the patient at risk for infections, bleeding, and severe fatigue. White blood cells are nonexistent, so they cannot fight infections, and patients may experience fevers and need antibiotics.

Low platelet counts can lead to bleeding, and platelet transfusions are common during this time. A low red blood cell count (called anemia) can also occur. The patient may look pale, feel tired, and need red blood cell transfusions. Many patients say the worst side effect is extreme fatigue. Just getting out of bed is a chore.

Patients also deal with the side effects of chemotherapy. These include diarrhea, nausea and vomiting, hair loss, fever, chills, decreased appetite, and mouth sores. Every patient is different, and it is hard to tell who will have which side effects. The chemotherapy drugs used before the transplant can vary; some medications are more likely to cause certain side effects than others.

What is engraftment?

Engraftment is the point when the stem cells start doing their job, and blood cell counts start to come up. The first number doctors look for is the neutrophil count, the type of white blood cell most important in fighting infection. The care team will watch the neutrophil count, and when it reaches a specific level, the patient can go home. The time until engraftment varies but is often between nine to twelve days. The red blood cell and platelet counts can take a few weeks to get back to a normal range.

I spent seventeen days in the hospital and fourteen days after my stem cell transplant.

CHAPTER 1

Growing Up Christian

I can do everything through him who gives me strength.
—Philippians 4:13

I imagine there are children who grow up thinking they can conquer the world, do anything they want, and be anyone they want. They dream big, set lofty goals, and work hard. I was not that kind of child.

I was the kind of child who preferred the background over the limelight. I had dreams, but I didn't share them with anyone, and I had no real plans for achieving them. (For example, during third grade [1968–1969], I recall that I wanted to be an airline hostess. I'd never ridden in a plane and had no idea what hostesses did, only that it sounded glamorous and different from my current life.)

I grew up in a Christian home with married parents and four younger brothers. We attended two church services on Sunday and one on Wednesday evenings. Most of my parents' friends were from church, and most of the socializing we did as a family was with these families.

Almost all the families included four or five children. However, I did not go to school with any of these children, and I always felt I was two different people, one person for school and one for church.

I was the oldest of all the children of my parent's friends, and this gave me a bit of clout and confidence. When we were together,

I was able to be more outgoing and to have the kind of childish fun that I did not feel at home or in school. As I moved into my teenage years, I desperately wanted to let go of being two different people; I was unsure how to do this.

As a teenager, I believed in God. I believed that Jesus was His son, that He was born a babe in a manger, and that He walked on earth for thirty-three years. I believed He died on the cross to cover my sins and the sins of the world and that He arose three days later and ascended into heaven. I believed that He would return one day to rescue the saved from the atrocities that would befall those left on earth.

These lessons were taught through Sunday school, vacation Bible school, and weekly church sermons. But I didn't see how these beliefs and ideas worked for me at school. I didn't have any school friends who had beliefs like mine.

Between my sophomore and junior years of high school, my family moved homes, requiring me to change schools. This might be the answer to my dilemma. I was being given a fresh start; I could be who I wanted to be because no one would know the difference. I wanted to be more outgoing, develop friendships, and have fun—to be more like the me I was when I was with my church friends.

I subconsciously decided that I would be different at my new school. Not only would I be more outgoing and fun, but I would not hide my religious beliefs. It is highly possible that I would have failed in this endeavor if not for two people who entered my life in the fall of 1977 as I began my junior year of high school in a new community.

Katrina[4] was a young woman from Germany; she was petite in stature, eighteen years old, with deep red hair and oozing compassion. She was an exchange student, and we were her host family. She was a Christian, not just a *go-to-church-on-Sunday* Christian, but she loved and lived for Christ. For some reason, this was a novel idea to me, and we spent many hours conversing about what it meant to have a personal relationship with Jesus.

---

[4] This is a pseudonym.

Kat showed me how to read the Bible and remember verses, and she shared her personal journals with me and encouraged me to keep a journal of my thoughts and feelings, about verses I resonated with, and questions I had. Through this process, I gravitated to the verse in Philippians 4:13,

> I can do everything through him who gives me strength.

This verse became my mantra, and it has comforted and sustained me throughout my life.

Jacob[5] also entered my life in the fall of 1977. He was a classmate at my new school, and we were both on the college prep track, so we saw each other multiple times per day. Jacob was Catholic; his family was devout to their faith. As he and I began a friendship and then a romantic relationship, we talked often about Christianity broadly and the tenets of my Protestant and his Catholic faiths. I had never had a school friend who cared about religion and was willing to talk about it. This was a huge turning point for my faith journey.

In the third grade, I had a teacher who encouraged me, told me I was smart, and challenged me to go to college, but I wasn't sure about my future as no one in my family had gone to college. However, after moving schools, talking with Kat and Jacob, and getting accepted into several state universities, I had a better sense of my future. Armed with my mantra and lofty dreams, at the age of seventeen, I went to college to study education—I was going to be a teacher.

Note: I became a middle and high school math year and taught for fourteen years before going on to earn a master's and PhD and teach at the college level.

---

[5] Also a pseudonym.

Laura and her grandchildren less than two
weeks before the neurologic event

CHAPTER 2

Something's Not Right Here

So do not fear, for I am with you; do not be dismayed,
for I am your God. I will strengthen you and help you;
I will uphold you with my righteous right hand.
—Isaiah 41:10

I learned that courage was not the absence of fear, but
the triumph over it. The brave man is not he who does
not feel afraid, but he who conquers that fear.
—Nelson Mandela

There were signs that something was wrong with me as early as 2017. In June of that year, I accompanied a group of college students to Liverpool, England. It was my seventh such trip since 2007, and I was eager to show the UK to a new group of future educators.

In the UK, we walk a lot. We walk to meals, to schools, and to hangout spots. In past years, I have logged twenty thousand steps in one day, especially in London. In June of 2017, I walked as much as I usually do, but my legs started to bother me a great deal. From mid-calf to my ankle, on both legs, I started to notice a red, blotchy rash, and the rash was hot to the touch.

I visited the chemist (similar to a pharmacist in the US), and he suggested that I had some sort of allergic reaction that caused the rash, and he sold me some ointment. While the ointment did help with making the rash less noticeable and less warm to the touch, the tingling/numb feeling in my legs and feet continued throughout my trip.

The next incident occurred on a camping trip that same summer with a friend and her children. One day, we took the ferry to Mackinaw Island, a great tourist attraction for Michigan, situated between the upper and lower peninsulas. We had decided we were going to ride bikes around the island. There are no motor vehicles allowed on Mackinaw Island, and it is common for tourists to ride bikes around the island. I had done this ride many times earlier in my life.

After we had each been fitted with a rental bike and donned helmets, we slowly navigated all the walkers, bikers, and horses to get out of town so we would have a more open space to ride.

As we got to a long straight stretch near Lake Huron on the southeast side of the island, we pulled over so that my friend could talk to her children about her expectations for how far ahead they could ride.

At that point, I told her that I was not feeling confident about riding the bike. I felt off balance, and I was hesitant to continue. She looked at the seat and had me extend my legs to see if the seat was at the right height. She convinced me that I could do it; I had ridden bikes many times in my life, and she was sure it would come back to me as we got rolling.

A few minutes later, her oldest son went to pass me and his back wheel struck my front wheel. I struggled to right myself, and I applied the brake. However, I was unable to regain control of the bike, and I careened into the grassy, weedy ditch. As I did, I fell off the bike and smacked my face into the ground.

When I sat up, I realized blood was running down my face, and I had intense pain from the middle of my face. After a huge to-do involving a bike safety officer, an emergency radio call, and an ambulance (the only motor vehicle allowed on the island), I ended up in a small hospital where I was diagnosed with a broken nose and a concussion. Needless to say, our relaxing day on Mackinaw Island came to an end.

As I recuperated over the next few days at the campsite near the island, my friend and her kids went on hikes and fishing outings. I felt like I was holding them back and putting a damper on their vacation. I started to blame my health issues on the fact that I needed to lose weight, that I had not stayed in shape, and that I was just getting too old to engage in these sorts of activities.

When we returned from the camping trip, I contacted my former personal trainer and set up training sessions again. When she heard about my bike accident and tried to get a baseline on my capabilities and strengths, she asserted that I was still suffering from a concussion because I became dizzy and light-headed when I did anything that required me to bend over. As we worked together over the next couple of months, she was cautious not to push me to the point of passing out.

In late August, just before school began, I had an episode of dizziness, loss of balance, and light-headedness that became so intense that my trainer took me to the ER at the local hospital. After some testing and discussion with doctors, it was suggested that I might have vertigo, and I was sent home to follow up with my primary care doctor and, most likely, an ENT (ear, nose, and throat specialist). This was only the beginning of many potential diagnoses from many specialists.

I started succumbing to the fear of never knowing what was wrong with me. I feared that maybe nothing was wrong with me and that I was imagining that I felt bad. Like the quote by Nelson Mandela, and the bible verse from Isaiah that opened this chapter, I was beginning to let my fear take hold. I was getting into a dark place, and the journey was only beginning.

CHAPTER 3

Experiencing COVID as a Teacher

A single sunbeam is enough to drive away many shadows.
—Saint Francis of Assisi

I am a professor of education at a small liberal arts Christian college in the Midwest. When COVID hit our campus in March of 2020, like most of America, my life changed drastically. One day I was teaching on campus, attending meetings, advising students, and engaging in the life of a faculty at a busy undergraduate residential college. The next day, like so many others, I was stuck at home. From March 12 through the end of the school year, I taught from home, utilizing Zoom and Google Meets and learning many new techniques and technologies to meet the needs of my students.

Serendipitously, it was also in March 2020 that I welcomed a young dog into my home. Kiki was abandoned and living on the streets of Texas when I found her on a rescue website, and I adopted her. We got well acquainted while I was teaching at home, and I grew to appreciate the time I spent walking her and having a listening ear as I talked myself down from panic many times.

During the following school year (2020 to 2021), I delivered a hybrid of instruction types—some in-person, with masks, social distance, and other safety protocols; and some virtual (Zoom) instruction. Because I had the flexibility to adjust my schedule, I could continue teaching because when I was not feeling well, I could switch to a virtual format.

My not feeling well meant I was dizzy and light-headed, and I lost my balance easily. I began to use the wall or furniture to walk around my home. But because I was teaching virtually, I could do this fairly easily.

Near the end of April, about four weeks before the end of the spring semester, I had an acute neurologic event (more about this in the next chapter), was hospitalized for five days, and did not return to teaching in that school year. Several colleagues stepped up and finished my classes for me, and I am incredibly thankful.

Having a supportive work family, colleagues, staff, and students gave me one less thing to worry about as I faced uncertainty about what lay ahead for me. These people (and Kiki) were my sunbeams during this dark time and absolutely brought light into my life.

Laura and Kiki right before her adoption

CHAPTER 4

The Neurologic Event

When all I see is the battle, you see my victory
When all I see is the mountain, you see a mountain moved
And as I walk through the shadow, your love surrounds me
There's nothing to fear now for I am safe with You

So when I fight, I'll fight on my knees
With my hands lifted high
Oh God, the battle belongs to You
And every fear I lay at Your feet
I'll sing through the night
Oh God, the battle belongs to You
—Lyrics from "Battle Belongs"
by Phil Wickham[6]

It was a Monday in April of 2021. I sat at my kitchen table preparing for my 1:00 p.m. secondary education class. We were nearing the end of the semester, and I was thinking about how I would support my students who were nearing their breaking points at this time of the semester. Most of them would be student teaching in the fall

---

[6] Lyrics.com, "Battle Belongs Lyrics," STANDS4 LLC, 2023, accessed June 15, 2023. https://www.lyrics.com/lyric/38627023/Phil+Wickham/Battle+Belongs.

semester, and this was their last push to complete all the program requirements; needless to say, they were stressed.

I'm still not sure what happened next, but all of a sudden, I felt weird. I did not, and still do not know, how to describe it; I felt like something had just changed in my body. I stood up gingerly, accustomed to regular feelings of dizziness when I stood. When I felt no dizziness, I began walking toward the bathroom and immediately ran into the wall in the hallway. I hit the wall with my shoulder, and my eyes welled with tears. I proceeded down the hall toward the bathroom, this time keeping my hand on the wall to steady myself.

When I got to the bathroom, I grabbed the sink with both hands and waited for nausea and dizziness to subside (these were both common occurrences in the last couple of years, so I didn't think too much of it.). When my stability was once again established, I let go of the sink and proceeded to the toilet. As I was on my way down to the seat, I realized, too late, that I was off center of the seat, and I fell hard to the ground beside the toilet.

I cried outright this time of the pain of hitting the wall, the floor, and now the toilet, and I didn't know what was happening to me. Once I had calmed down and used the toilet, I walked precariously and, with the wall as my guide, grabbed my phone and rested in my recliner.

I knew from my dad having a ministroke a few years prior that losing equilibrium might be a sign of a stroke, so I googled and read about the signs of a stroke. I could smile normally, I could say my ABCs, I was not confused, and I was no longer feeling dizzy. Not sure of what to do, I canceled class for the afternoon and took a nap.

When I woke, I felt fine. I proceeded to make something to eat and went back to class preparation. I talked to a friend that evening and told her what had happened, and we collectively decided that it was just part of my ongoing dizziness and other health problems and that nothing else was wrong. In hindsight, I should have turned to God and prayed for insight on how to proceed with this battle.

The next morning, as I sat up in bed, I was so dizzy that I almost fell out of bed. I tried to walk to the bathroom and staggered to the right, unable to walk normally. The left side of my body felt heavy and sluggish, and it did not want to cooperate. As soon as 8:00 a.m. came, I called my doctor's office. The nurse asked me some questions—similar to what I had noticed from my search for stroke symptoms.

Then she had me look in the mirror and raise both my arms straight in front of me—my left arm would not stay level, and each time I tried to bring it up, it just fell back down. When I shared this with her, she told me to go immediately to urgent care or an ER. Oh, and to *not* drive myself. She said I should call an ambulance if I couldn't get someone to drive me in the next hour. I began to worry, and this time, I began to pray.

A friend arrived about thirty minutes later and took me to the urgent care close to my home. I was having trouble walking, and when the urgent-care doctor talked to me for only a few minutes, he told me I needed to go to the ER. He felt I needed a CT scan because I was exhibiting signs of a stroke. My worry increased as did the fervor of my prayers. In my mind, I was facing a battle of unknown parameters and depth, and I needed God to step in. Obviously, this is easy to say, but it is not so easy to let go.

When I got to the ER, the urgent-care doc had already faxed my information and his tentative diagnosis, so they were ready for me. After the preliminary taking of my vitals and getting me into a gown, I was taken for a CT scan. My friend had to leave, so I was alone, waiting to hear what the scan revealed. I had not called my children or parents, as I had no diagnosis yet, and I did not want to worry them unnecessarily. Sitting alone in the hospital, waiting to hear the results of my CT, unending and unfettered prayers streamed upward.

About fifteen minutes after the scan, the ER doctor came in. He said they would admit me because there were some white spots on my brain scan, and he did not know what they were. His tentative diagnosis was that I had suffered a ministroke.

As I waited to be admitted and taken to a room in the hospital, I called my kids and my parents, and I texted my friend and my department chair. I continued to pray—for strength, comfort, and the doctors' wisdom but also for my family and friends who were likely worrying as well.

I cannot say that my worry had decreased, but knowing that at least one doctor realized there was something wrong with me and wanted to conduct further tests to find answers was a relief. At the same time, I felt calm and peace that God was now taking over this battle.

Laura with her children Chad and Megan less than two weeks before the neurologic event

CHAPTER 5

Still No Answers

The Lord himself goes before you and will be with you. He will never leave you nor forsake you. Do not be afraid, do not be discouraged.
—Deuteronomy 31:8

It was my fifth day in Holland Hospital, and I was ready to go home. Since I had been admitted following a neurologic event, which might have been a ministroke, I had undergone a huge number of tests as the hospital neurologists tried to figure out what was wrong with me. I have to admit I was discouraged.

After a second CT with contrast, it was determined that I had not had a ministroke. Still, because I had been admitted as a probable stroke victim, I underwent the stroke protocol by the hospital nurses every four hours. It involved holding up my arms while my eyes were closed, squeezing the nurse's fingers, pushing against the nurse with my hands and feet, and answering mundane questions designed to assess my physical and cognitive functions.

As each test was performed and no diagnosis emerged, the doctors remained stumped and began to speculate about what might be happening to me. They were especially concerned with the weakness and tingling on the left side of my body and the fact that I could not walk on my own because I kept falling and leaning to the right.

They ordered multiple MRIs (head/neck, and all three sections of my spine), with and without contrast, an echocardiogram, a lumbar puncture, a nose/throat exploration, a temporal artery biopsy, and lots of blood work. One aspect of my blood work, the ESR (sedentary rate), continued to be in abnormal ranges. The doctors hypothesized that I had inflection or inflammation somewhere in my body; the problem was that they could not determine where the infection was.

Across the five days, doctors ruled out many things: MS (multiple sclerosis), ALS (amyotrophic lateral sclerosis), HIV, syphilis, herpes, Parkinson's disease, Huntington's disease, and GBS (Guillain-Barré syndrome). I did not have a brain or spinal column injury, but I had suffered some sort of acute neurologic event that caused significant nerve damage.

I left the hospital with a tentative diagnosis of atypical migraines and a treatment plan of steroids, blood pressure meds, diet, rest, and low stress. I was also to keep a diary of daily weight, blood pressure, and temperature and to note when I experienced more dizziness and headaches. The suggestion was that the migraines might be brought on by diet or stress, and keeping a detailed log might help the doctors figure this out.

Oh, I also left with an assistive device as I could not walk independently without falling.

When I met with my primary care doctor a few days after my discharge, she recommended that I seek a secondary diagnosis at the neurology center in Grand Rapids. I also asked her about Mayo Clinic, and she enthusiastically endorsed my query about making an appointment at Mayo.

I attended physical and occupational therapy all summer, seeking rides from my colleagues and friends until I was cleared to drive. When I began PT, I was using a walker; as time progressed, I moved to a trekking pole, and finally, I walked on my own. I learned how to do typical household chores in OT without falling or getting too tired.

I contacted the Mayo Clinic and set up appointments with the Department of Neurology for late September. I faced a summer of instability, unable to walk, wanting answers for what was wrong with me. I experienced humility that I had never been forced to confront; I grew physically and spiritually, but it was tough. My attitude and mood were at a low point, and I looked forward to going to Mayo Clinic to get long-awaited answers.

I tentatively made plans to begin my work as a full-time professor for the fall 2021 semester.

CHAPTER 6

In the Hospital Again

Oh, just one word, you calm the storm that surrounds me
Just one word, the darkness has to retreat
Oh, just one touch, I feel the presence of heaven
Just one touch, my eyes were opened to see
My heart can't help but believe

And just one word, you heal what's broken inside me
And just one word and You revive every dream
Just one touch, I feel the power of heaven
And just one touch, my eyes were opened to see
My heart can't help but believe

There's nothing that our God can't do
There's not a mountain that He can't move
Oh, praise the name that makes a way
There's nothing that our God can't do

—Music by Trevecca Worship
("There's Nothing That Our God Can't Do[7]")

---

[7] Lyrics.com, "There's Nothing That Our God Can't Do Lyrics," STANDS4 LLC, 2023, accessed June 15, 2023. https://www.lyrics.com/lyric-lf/2422891/ Trevecca+Worship/There%26%23039%3Bs+Nothing+That+Our+God+ Can%26%23039%3Bt+Do.

After my discharge from Holland Hospital in late April of 2021, I saw my primary care doctor. When I told her that the neurologists at the hospital were stumped about what was wrong with me, suggesting it might be complex migraines, she referred me to the neurology center in Grand Rapids for a second opinion.

Later that summer, in June, I met with Dr. C, a neurologist at the Hauenstein Neuroscience Center. My son accompanied me to this appointment. Dr. C was easy to talk to, he asked a lot of questions, he thoughtfully reflected upon my answers, and he conducted some of his own physical tests.

I had endured many of the same tests while I was in Holland Hospital: determining strength in my arms, hands, and legs and having a pin stuck into numerous body parts, including my back and spine. After Dr. C did the pin-poking test, he left the room rather abruptly.

When he returned, he said that he wanted to admit me to the hospital for further testing. He was new to the center, having only arrived that week from a twenty-five-year stint at the University of Michigan Hospital organization. He had to check with the nursing staff to find out how to do a direct admit.

He wanted to conduct his own MRIs and other tests to see if he could determine what was wrong. He had reviewed my test results and the doctor's notes from Holland Hospital and was not convinced that I had suffered from some sort of migraine.

After Dr. C worked through some red tape, I was admitted to St. Mary's Hospital in Grand Rapids, where I spent three days having MRIs of all three areas of my spine (cervical, thoracic, and lumbar) with contrast. I saw several neuro-specialists, answered a multitude of questions, and endured additional pin-poking tests as the doctors tried to determine what was wrong. After three days of tests and when none of the tests revealed a diagnosis, I was released.

After being discharged, I met with Dr. C again in his office at the Neuroscience Center. He was stymied. He claimed that in his twenty-five-plus years of practice, he had not seen a case like mine, and he had no idea what was going on with me. It was all I could do to hold back my tears.

I informed him that I already had an appointment at Mayo Clinic near the end of September, and he was excited about the prospect and made me promise to let him know what they found out. The best news was that Dr. C felt confident that the doctors at Mayo Clinic would figure out what was wrong with me. That was completely uplifting, and I praised God for the potential that the future might hold.

CHAPTER 7

Finally, a Diagnosis

I think I know what's going on with you.
—Dr. S, Hematologist (August 2021)

When my primary care doctor heard that the neurologist group in Grand Rapids had no diagnosis, she ordered many blood tests. When the proteins in my blood showed extreme abnormalities, she sent me to a hematologist.

After a quick tap on the exam room door, a slender, professionally dressed, young woman entered. She introduced herself as Dr. S and proceeded to make the above announcement.

I had heard numerous specialists over the previous three years say almost the opposite, claiming to have run the tests, reviewed the labs, and ruled out the most sinister of ailments. But in the end, no one could provide me with a diagnosis.

I was unsure I had heard her correctly, and I think I must have stared at Dr. S with my mouth agape as those were the words I had coveted for so long. Her words continued as she introduced the word *amyloidosis*, a rare blood disorder that can present itself differently in each patient (thereby making it hard to diagnose).

Her explanation was longer than what I noted here, but I think I was shocked. Much of what she described resonated with me, and as I listened, it seemed more and more likely that she actually did know what I had.

Dr. S explained that the first thing we had to do was confirm the diagnosis, which is usually done through a bone marrow biopsy. One was scheduled for the following week, in her office with no sedation; however, the results were inconclusive. A second biopsy was scheduled at a local hospital where I was sedated, but the results were inconclusive.

Earlier in the summer, I had scheduled an appointment at Mayo Clinic for further exploration following the neurology problems I had experienced for a few years. When I shared my plans with Dr. S, she recommended that I keep that appointment but add hematology to the visit.

I left that appointment feeling a glimmer of hope that had for so long eluded me. While I had no idea if this was actually my diagnosis or what the treatment plan might entail, having someone who thought they knew what was going on with me was an answer to prayers.

CHAPTER 8

"I need help"

*Keep the faith. The most amazing things in life tend to
happen right when you're about to give up hope.*
—Unknown

As the summer of 2021 ended, I was uplifted by the potential diagnosis and my upcoming visit to the Mayo Clinic at the end of September. I also began my thirty-ninth school year as an educator.

My work began in August when I co-led a three-day workshop for new faculty and a two-day professional development for the members of my department. At the end of the month, classes began, and I resumed my teaching assignments with accommodations[8]. I had planned to take two weeks off at the end of September/beginning of October to attend Mayo Clinic. I had arranged for colleagues to cover my three classes for the two-week period.

Dr. S prescribed dexamethasone[9] to me in early September 2021. She was fairly sure of her diagnosis of amyloidosis, even though both of the bone marrow biopsies had been inconclusive. She hoped this drug would alleviate some of my discomforts, especially the swelling

---

[8] I taught only two days a week. I was assigned the same classroom for all three classes and that room was as close to my office as possible. I attended all department and committee meetings via Zoom or Google Meet.

[9] A steroid designed to reduce inflammation: it's also used to treat many blood disorders.

in my left leg and foot. She also noted that steroids are often used for treating blood disorders, like amyloidosis.

She put me on a high dosage for a ten-day period (40 mg per day), knowing that I was headed to Mayo at the end of the month. For the first few days on the medication, I did not notice any changes in my leg's swelling or experience any side effects. However, it was not long before the drug made me nauseous, caused me to sweat, and gave me constipation.

On September 21, my last week of teaching, I arrived on campus for my 8:30 a.m. class before leaving for Mayo. I began to set up the classroom and make final preparations when I had a huge rush of heat and a nauseous feeling that indicated I was about to vomit. I rushed to the bathroom, barely making it in time, to throw up. I washed my face and mouth with paper towels that I had wettened. After a few minutes, I left the bathroom and sat on a bench outside in the hallway.

I tried to calm myself down to finish prep and teach my class, but I could not. I was shaky, alternating between shivers and hot flashes, and I was almost afraid to stand up. Finally, I stumbled to the closest colleague's office and sat down. "I need help," was all I managed to say. Several colleagues stepped in as I sat and sobbed, took care of the students waiting for me in class, gathered my belongings, and eventually, two of them drove me home.

That was the last day I went to campus. The dexamethasone had kicked my butt, and I spent most of the rest of the week feeling like crap and napping when I was not vomiting or sweating.

Once again, several colleagues stepped into my classes and finished the semester. My classes for the spring 2022 semester were reassigned to other faculty, and I went on short-term and then long-term disability.

In April 2021, after being released from the hospital, when I could not walk, one of my students stepped up and offered to come every day to walk Kiki. He continued to do that throughout the fall and spring semesters, even though he was student teaching.

All my students supported me throughout the school year, sending me emails, notes, and cards and offering their prayers and encouragement. Some recounted stories of family members or friends who had experienced similar health situations and had positive outcomes.

I had mixed emotions when my son came to pick me up to go to Mayo a few days later—happy because I thought I would get some answers about my health but anxious because I couldn't image riding twelve hours in a car when I was feeling ill. However, I did feel uplifted by my students, family members, and colleagues. I also felt God's hands holding me tightly.

CHAPTER 9

The Mayo Clinic

When I am afraid, I will trust in you.
—Psalm 56:3

In late September of 2021, my son drove me to Rochester, Minnesota, where I had scheduled several appointments at the Mayo Clinic. When I first made the appointment in June of that year, I scheduled with the Department of Neurology as that was the best guess for where answers about my health issues originated. When I met Dr. S, and she diagnosed amyloidosis, I added additional appointments with the Department of Hematology at Mayo.

While many folks might immediately think of the Mayo Clinic when something is wrong, it was my last resort for me. I had been to so many specialists and had so many medical tests over a four-year period that I was beginning to think that I would never know what was wrong with me and that I was destined to be *sick* for the rest of my life.

If you have ever been to Mayo Clinic, you know how amazing the doctors and technicians are, how organized they are, and how you are treated with respect in every aspect of your visit. I am so thankful for the kindness, professionalism, and knowledge I felt during the twelve days I spent in Rochester.

While at Mayo, I met with neurology, hematology, cardiology, and endocrinology doctors and was administered lots of tests, including regular blood work. One of the tests confirmed Dr. S's initial diagnosis. I had amyloidosis.

I learned more about the disease—a rare blood disorder in which some of my blood cells had gone rogue and moved around my body causing havoc. It became clear from the tests that I had quite a bit of neurologic damage from the amyloids. And given that the neurologic symptoms were what I noticed first, they likely began their attacks in 2017.

Doctors at Mayo also discovered that I had cardiac and kidney damage from the amyloids. They tried to get me in to see a doctor in nephrology (a kidney doctor), but there were no openings, so I promised I would consult with a kidney doctor as soon as I got home.

I left Mayo with a confirmed diagnosis, more knowledge about the disease, and a treatment plan in place. I had been praying and coveting prayers from almost everyone I knew for a diagnosis, and I returned home feeling blessed and hopeful for the first time in a long time.

Our God is good, and He had been faithful, and I was so blessed.

CHAPTER 10

The C Word

And if I asked you to name all the things that you love,
how long would it take for you to name yourself?
—Sana Dabbas[10]

Sometimes I find the easiest way to process what's happening to me is to write. I drafted this poem on September 4, 2021, after I'd had my consultation with Dr. S, but before I went to Mayo Clinic. I revisited and revised the poem on January 6, 2022, when I was halfway through my chemo treatments.

The C Word

For me, the C word
Is not cancer,
But chemo.

Hearing multiple docs
Tell me I need chemo
Prompts me to ask
Do I have cancer?

---

[10] Sana Dabbas is a social media influencer.

LAURA PARDO

No, is the response,
but the treatment
For amyloidosis is
Chemo.

Any chemicals
Put into one's body
For the sole purpose
Of killing something
In the body
Is chemotherapy.
(Explanation by hematology fellow at Mayo Clinic)

So now I know.

But
I don't know how to
Process
Feel
Understand.

Sometimes I'm fine
Journaling or scrapbooking,
Playing iPhone games,
Coloring or binge watching
Worst Cooks in America
Or British true crime.

Sometimes I'm sad
Wallowing in self-pity
And loneliness

What do I say
When asked how I'm doing?

I CAN DO HARD THINGS

I honestly don't know how I'm doing.
How would you be doing if someone told you
You don't have cancer
But you need chemotherapy?
And a stem cell/bone marrow transplant?
But only if you respond positively
To the chemo.

Am I afraid?
Sure—who wouldn't be?

Am I dealing with it?
Really? What does that even mean?

What are my plans?
For what?
(I think I'll have a salad for lunch)

After my hospitalization
In April,
I had a premonition
Supported by blood and urine tests
Whose numbers fell
Outside
The normal ranges
that
Whatever had been plaguing me
For over three years
Was not good.

But really, it wasn't that hard to deduce.
And now I know.

I have amyloidosis
A rare blood disease
I'm in stage 2

I'm in chemo
Once a week for a minimum of
Four months
Waiting to get a stem cell transplant
Which is the only respite
To get my body
Back to "normal"
(Which after living in a COVID world takes on
a whole new meaning)

My amyloids are strong
They are attackers.

They've attacked my nervous system
causing peripheral neuropathy
On the left side of my body
Leaving numbness, tingling, and lack of sensation
In my left foot, leg, thigh, and hip.

They've attacked my nephrotic system
Stage 1 kidney disease with
Nephrotic syndrome.
Basically, I pee out every protein.
In my body, causing edema
In my legs, stomach, face, and neck.

They've attacked my cardiovascular system
Off the chart triglycerides and cholesterol levels
Widening of my sternum (not sure what that means)
And increasing my chances of having a stroke

There's a question as to whether
They've attacked my skin
As the weird growths I've acquired
On my face over the last few years
Might be amyloids.

I CAN DO HARD THINGS

But I can't go to one more specialist
(Physically I could, but mentally I'm done)
And if they are amyloids,
The chemo might kill them.

It's also unclear if these
Nasty amyloids have anything to do
With my thyroid problems
Either way, my treatment options
Remain the same
Treat the hypothyroidism
And treat the amyloids.

But,
And this is a big *but*;
I'm not alone on this journey.
Not only do I have
Awesome friends,
A loving family,
A supportive life group,
Inspiring colleagues,
But

I serve an awesome God
And He is good
And merciful
And gracious
And I feel His healing hand
Not only on my body,
But also on my heart.

And in the end
What matters most
Is that I have a personal relationship
With my Savior
And I can say

With confidence
And the faith of my fathers,
that
"God's got this!"

CHAPTER 11

The Treatment Plan

But those who hope in the Lord will renew their strength.
They will soar on wings like eagles; they will run and
not grow weary, they will walk and not be faint.
—Isaiah 40:31

The doctors at Mayo provided me with a treatment plan, and when I returned from Mayo Clinic, I met with Dr. S, my hematologist at the Cancer Center in my hometown. I also met with a social worker, a financial planner, a counselor, and a registered nurse. I was provided with many resources to help me understand what the chemotherapy process would look like for me. It was a bit overwhelming; however, I was glad that my treatment plan was finally going to be implemented. I had waited so long for a diagnosis and to hear what the treatment would consist of.

From this team, I learned that I would receive chemotherapy once a week for four to six cycles. A cycle is four weeks, so I was looking at sixteen to twenty-four treatments. The goal of the chemo was to eradicate the amyloids that were wreaking havoc on my body. Once my blood labs showed that the amyloids were decreasing, I could be considered for a stem cell transplant.

My blood was drawn every Wednesday before the injections. The blood was analyzed for white blood cell counts, hemoglobin, platelets, and ANC (baby red blood cells). At the end of each cycle, additional tests were done to check my kidney and liver functions, my electrolytes, and the number of amyloids (by looking at the light chains within my blood cells).

My chemo consisted of a four-drug cocktail, the good news being that two of the drugs would be delivered orally and the other two through injections. This meant that I would not have to get a port, not have to have treatments through an IV, and my time at the center every week would be substantially less than I had first imagined.

Each Wednesday morning, I took five 4-mg tablets of dexamethasone and fourteen 50 mg tablets of cyclophosphamide. I also took a Tylenol, a Benadryl tablet, and anti-nausea medication as a preemptive measure for the potential side effects of the drugs.

At the center, I received two injections into my stomach; Velcade and Darzalex. The Velcade (also called dortezomib) was similar to any shot/vaccine; however, if the nurse pushed the drug too quickly, I experienced a great burning sensation at the site. Because I had different nurses across the five months, I had to remember to tell each one to administer the shot slowly. The couple of times that I forgot, thankfully, my dad remembered.

Darzalex (also called Daratumumab) consisted of a thick liquid and a much larger syringe. The drug had to be injected slowly, taking five to ten minutes to dispense the entire dose. Because there is so much liquid to inject, there's also something in the liquid that creates a pocket under my skin so that there is room for all the liquid, which can slowly be absorbed by my body.

This newer drug has only been used recently to treat blood disorders like amyloidosis and multiple myeloma. Research studies found that the addition of this drug made a great difference in the treatment working. This drug costs $14,000 for one dose; thankfully I have excellent insurance, and I did not have any out-of-pocket expenses for this drug or any part of my chemotherapy. I realized this was another way God had provided for me.

In addition to the four chemo drugs, I was placed on two antibiotics: a broad-spectrum medication and one to combat shingles and pneumonia. Because of the side effects of the drugs, I was encouraged to take Imodium AD for diarrhea, a stool softener for constipation, and Zofran for nausea as needed.

I ended up with twenty treatments; every Wednesday from mid-October to early March, my dad accompanied me to the Cancer and Hematology Center near my home. I experienced many side effects over the course of treatment; diarrhea, constipation, nausea, vomiting, dry mouth, dizziness, and my finger and toe nails began to split and peel. While my hair thinned, it did not fall out (that didn't happen until seventeen days after my transplant). My skin became thin and bruised easily, and any little bump or scratch hurt like I'd been stabbed.

However, knowing that this was the treatment regime that would bring me back my health and my life, I never questioned whether I should do it, even given the nasty side effects. As the prophet Isaiah noted, those who wait upon the Lord will reap the benefits; I had been waiting for a long time, and I was now ready to reap the benefits—to feel better and resume a healthy lifestyle.

Laura with her two youngest grandchildren three months posttransplant

CHAPTER 12

The Heroes in My Family

Family isn't an important thing, it's everything.
—Michael J. Fox

On every journey, one needs heroes for help with everything from menial household tasks to cheerleading and holding one up in love. My family fulfills these roles for me. In fact, they not only fulfill these roles but exceed them.

My children are in their thirties, with spouses and children of their own. They have jobs and busy lives and live several hours from me. However, they helped whenever and however they could, sending me goody packages, calling and FaceTiming, praying, and reassuring me that I was in God's hands.

My son Chad drove me to Mayo Clinic in late September, and he stayed with me for the twelve days that I met with doctors and had tests. He worked from our hotel room, but I know that leaving his wife and two children for almost two weeks was challenging, and I am forever grateful for their sacrifice.

My daughter called me several times a week, and her children made me cards and drew pictures; some of these are still on my refrigerator. One of the most meaningful messages was from then-seven-year-old Preston, my daughter Megan's oldest child. In perfect cursive, he wrote:

> from Preston to grandma
>
> Dear grandma
>
> I hope you have not been feeling to bad lately. I have been praying for you every day.
> I love you!

Chad's oldest, my only granddaughter, regularly wrote me letters, collaborated with me on shared stories through Google Docs, FaceTimed, and sent multiple homemade cards. These memories and artifacts are precious reminders of God's grace and faithfulness.

I am blessed that both of my parents are alive and that they live about thirty minutes away. Before my diagnosis, they regularly checked in with me and encouraged me to remember that God is faithful.

My Aunt Linda[11] called, texted, and visited when possible. Her strong faith and kind encouragement seemed to come when I needed it most. When I was a child, she had been my babysitter, and our relationship has always been special. I knew her prayers for me were constant and genuine.

Three of my four brothers are alive; one lives out of state, one lives out of the country, and one lives about thirty minutes away. However, they all checked on me regularly. They buoyed my spirits by recalling humorous experiences from our childhood, telling me about their own lives and families, and sending inspirational verses or quotes.

I cannot imagine how much more difficult this journey would have been without the love and support of my family.

---

[11] My dad's sister

Laura's parents with Megan's four boys

CHAPTER 13

The Blood Marrow Transplant Team

To get through the hardest journey and continue living, we need to take only one step at a time; but we must keep stepping.
—Chinese proverb

After five rounds of chemo, Dr. S felt that I was doing so well, the presence of amyloid light chains had decreased substantially, that I was ready to talk to the doctors at the Blood Marrow Transplant Unit (BMT) in Grand Rapids. This is the team of doctors who would conduct my stem cell transplant. Dr. S had brought my case to them, and they agreed to see me.

After meeting with the BMT group for an initial consultation, I met with even more doctors and specialists. I needed to be cleared and deemed healthy enough to undergo the transplant. I underwent another bone marrow biopsy, had an echocardiogram, and a lot more blood work. I saw a cardiologist, an allergist, a pulmonologist, and an ophthalmologist. Doctors I had been seeing regularly, a nephrologist, endocrinologist, neurologist, and even my dentist, had to sign off before the transplant process could proceed.

When each of those specialists had cleared me as healthy enough to undergo a stem cell transplant, I moved into the next step: preparing for harvesting my stem cells.

On the first day of April (2022), I was taught how to administer injections into my stomach. For each of the next five days, I gave myself three shots in my stomach. The drugs were to stimulate the growth of my stem cells so that when the harvest occurred, there would be a lot of new stem cells.

Four days later, I had a central line inserted into my chest to aid the harvest process. The next day, the doctors began the harvest. For two days, I was hooked up to a machine that pulled my blood out of one of the ports and forced the blood into a bowl-shaped device that spun and caused all the stem cells to be separated from the mature cells.

The stem cells went into an IV bag, and the remaining blood was put back into me through the other port. I also received platelets and electrolytes throughout the entire process.

My collection lasted six hours on two consecutive days. At the end of that time, the doctors had collected five bags of stem cells, over seven million stem cells that would be transplanted back into me in a few short weeks. Each bag was frozen as it was filled, and I was informed that they would remain frozen until the transplant.

The goal for the collection was to harvest twice as many stem cells as were deemed necessary for my transplant, in case I needed a second transplant in the coming months. I learned of this on the last day of collection; to be honest, it worried me a bit; this had never been mentioned by any of my doctors. But I had learned to put one foot in front of the other and to keep my hand firmly in God's.

For almost two weeks after the harvest, I was instructed to take it easy and to make plans for after I returned from the hospital. My house and furnishings had to be immaculately clean and things that could make me sick or cause an infection had to go. I had to remove things from my home (my house plants and my dog). I arranged for a deep clean from a local cleaning service, purchased and arranged for a new carpet in the bedrooms, and with my daughter, threw out outdated spices, condiments, and beauty and health products.

I also met with the BMT doctors, and they explained the transplant procedure and what would occur in the days after the transplant. As the time for my hospital stay drew close, I felt at peace; I was taking the next step in my journey back to health, and I was ready.

CHAPTER 14

The Transplant and The Smell

Sometimes the good things
Fade from my mind
Hide in the crevices
Gathering dust
Transforming into shadows
Blurring my focus.

Clearing the cobwebs
Could be as simple as
A shake of my head
Stimulating the neurons
To fire once more.

As if the simplicity
Of a head shake
Were all that was needed
To lift a foul mood
To recall blessings
To find the good things
Once more

—Laura Pardo

The first time I heard about dimethyl sulfoxide was from my nurse in the transplant unit in the days before my transplant. She explained that this drug was a cryopreservative and had been used to preserve my stem cells as they were frozen and put into storage at the time of collection.

The nurse explained that this preservative had an odor, some patients said it smelled like creamed corn, and others thought it was metallic, but every patient was aware of the smell. She further explained that anyone who entered my room in the first few days posttransplant would smell it but that I would get used to it quickly, which should not bother me.

I was admitted to the hospital for the transplant two days before the actual transplant. There were several blood tests they had to perform, they pumped me with electrolytes and mentally prepared me for what was to come. The day before the transplant, I received a dose of chemo through the port that had been installed in my chest a day before I was admitted to the hospital. The transplant would proceed the following day.

I admit that I had completely forgotten what the nurse had warned me about the smell, and during the transplant, which spanned two days, I did not notice any kind of smell. However, the next morning as I was eating my breakfast, I thought there was something wrong with the pancakes or the syrup, there was a terrible smell/taste. I mentioned it to the nurse tech when she asked why I was not eating, and she posited that I was likely smelling the preservative coming from my own body. I asked her if she could smell it, and she replied that she could.

Over the next few days, the smell intensified, and I could smell it evaporating from my skin when I'd exhale. It didn't smell like creamed corn but rather something metallic and rotten. It made most of the food I tried to eat taste disgusting, including chocolate.

During my seventeen-day hospital stay, I received letters and cards daily. Along with the cards, I also received a great deal of chocolate, really good chocolate (See's, Ghirardelli, Godiva), as those who know me well knew I really liked chocolate. And I enjoyed the chocolate for a day or two, but when the preservative smell kicked in,

I couldn't eat the chocolate. In fact, the smell was so bad, and the chocolate so revolting that I sent it all home with my dad.

While the smell lessened as my stay in the hospital ended, and I was recuperating at home, it never left completely. Certain foods, medications, coffee, and other events bring that smell right back to me, and I can get nauseous quickly when the smell hits me. The worst thing has been being unable to eat chocolate and drink coffee—two things I really enjoyed pretransplant. I believe that in my mind, chocolate is associated with those first days after transplant when the smell was overwhelming.

Even ninety days posttransplant, there were times when the smell was just as vivid and real to me as it was in the days immediately after the transplant. I hope that someday I'll get joy out of chocolate and coffee again and will not be able to recall that smell.

CHAPTER 15

Humility

*Humility is not denying your strengths, humility
is being honest about your weaknesses.*
—Rick Warren

I was sitting in my hospital room, naked from the waist down. I was crying, not the hysterical sobbing of someone out of control, not the agonizing cry that emerges from real pain, but the tears running down my face, in despair, and lamenting my life as it was currently kind of crying.

On one hand, I wished the nurse would walk in; she could help me and reassure me and that would be that. I was supposed to conserve my energy for things that matter, and this was something for which I need not waste energy. But my stubborn side didn't want anyone to see me like this; I'm independent and can do hard things. For goodness' sake, I'm a grown-up woman. I should be able to put on my own adult diaper!

This occurred thirteen days posttransplant and was precipitated by the following event. I had not had a bowel movement for ten days posttransplant, which worried my doctors. Therefore, I was given both a stool softener and a laxative. Let's just say they worked. This would have been fine except that I did not make it to the toilet before my bowels opened. As if this weren't humiliating enough, I had to clean up my bottom and leave my soiled belongings on the bathroom floor. Hence, me sitting in a chair trying to put on my *brief*[12] and my last clean pair of yoga pants.

You may wonder why I did not call for the nurse to end my misery. The sad truth was that the call button was on the remote on the bed, which would require me to stand up and walk to the bed with no pants on. Now this might be okay if I could be confident that no one would walk in the room to catch me like this, but people would come in and out of my room all day, usually without a knock or with a simultaneous knock and entry.

So I persisted, trying to stop my tears as I struggled to get my legs into the brief and then my yoga pants. When the nurse entered later, she found me in the chair, dressed, and surprised when I told her about my *accident* and my subsequent efforts to clean up. I did not come clean with her about how taxing the event had been for me.

Needless to say, I still have much work to do in the area of humility.

____

[12] The nurse's kind name for adult diapers

Laura's sixty-first birthday with Chad's
children six months posttransplant

CHAPTER 16

Posttransplant

*To trust God in the light is nothing, but to
trust Him in the dark—that is faith.*
— C. H. Spurgeon[13]

It was two days past the transplant, and I was at a low point. My white blood cells, hemoglobin, platelets, and ANC (baby stem cells) were nonexistent. I was feeling extremely tired, my stomach was upset, I was lonely, and I had no appetite. The nurses tried to get me to eat chicken broth or crackers or applesauce, and I tried, but the smell of the preservative was overwhelming my senses.

I sent a group text that morning to my family and friends.

> Last night was rough. Diarrhea, dizziness, nausea. I'm also now a fall risk, so I can't go to the bathroom without a nurse. I've already set off the bed alarm twice. No appetite because of the preservatives with the stem cells. Horrible taste in my mouth—hoping that ends soon. Pray for me to stay calm and remember that this is temporary.

---

[13] Charles Spurgeon was a preacher at the beginning of the nineteenth century.

I struggled to stay optimistic, and I needed to remind myself that I had to go through the night before the daylight. My family and friends responded with encouragement, love, prayers, and other notes of support. One message from my brother Joel, five days after the transplant, meant a lot to me. In part, he wrote:

> I once heard Tony Dungy (NFL coach) talk about his battle with cancer. He talked about how he had to remind himself to live in the vision, not the circumstance. In his mind, he was coaching again, doing things with his family again, and being normal again. What a testimony he now has! He tells his story to encourage others.

As I reflected on and prayed about this over the next few days, I began to change my outlook on the future. I decided to list the things I wanted to resume when I was healthy again—things that had slipped from my life as I dealt with deteriorating health, physical weakness, and depression.

- Resume grandma camps each summer.[14]
- Spend time with my parents and brothers.
- Attend birthday parties and other holiday gatherings with my kids and grandkids.[15]
- Resume traveling, to conferences, to Liverpool[16], and to get away locations for rest and relaxation.

---

[14] For the previous three summers, I had designed a grandma camp for the older grandkids where they would come one or two at a time, and we would have a fun, jam-packed week. We'd go to the zoo, the beach, do some shopping and crafting, and make our favorite meals.

[15] Because of COVID and then my disease, I had not traveled to my children's homes for several years. This was really hard for me, and while FaceTime helped some, I missed being with my kids and grandkids in person.

[16] Since 2007, I had traveled to Liverpool, UK, in the summer, with a group of students from Hope College. During COVID, and then my disease, I had not been a part of the trip for four years.

- Teach! Research! Write![17]

I found this exercise both practical and inspiring. I have revisited this list several times since I originally wrote it, not to change anything but to be reminded of the potential in my life moving forward.

Joel also sent me a link to a song called "The Story I'll Tell" that he had recently heard at his church the previous two weeks. As I read the lyrics and listened to the song, I was reminded that God is always with me and that He has been faithful throughout my life, and now was not the time for doubt.

The lyrics describe the feeling of hopelessness for what is going on at the moment and remind us to look ahead beyond our current despair. The writer focuses on the testimony we will give in the future when we look back and see that God was with us throughout the journey. The song reminded me of the desolation and frustration I had felt for several years as my health declined and doctors could not provide clear answers. I was excited about the future, to be able to share my journey with others, to realize all the places and times that God's hand was in my life and that He's the one who brought me through.

---

[17] These are the professional activities that have compelled me forward in my career, and I miss the intellectual, relational, and creative parts of my life.

Laura with Megan's four boys ten months
posttransplant. On our way to church.

CHAPTER 17

Giving and Receiving

Carry each other's burdens, and in this way,
you will fulfill the law of Christ.
—Galatians 6:2

Surround yourself with people who are going to lift you higher.
—Oprah Winfrey

I've learned from this journey that having people who love you is a gift beyond measure, especially if those people can lift you up in prayer.

For most of my adult life, I was a giver, putting those in my life above my own needs. This is typical of mothers; even after my children were grown, I still found ways to help others. But the one thing I did not do was ask others to help me.

It was not that I thought others could not help me. I believe that I needed to prove my worth by giving and serving; being selfless was my self-imposed mantra.

I endured getting sick, feeling bad most of the time, going to doctor appointments and medical tests, and experiencing intense fatigue, all while trying to be strong and selfless. It did not work; I could not continue on my own. One of the hardest things I had to do was ask for help.

My colleagues and the members of my life group from my church offered their help immediately upon hearing of my hospitalization in April of 2021. Since I could not walk on my own when I returned home, I had to rely on these folks to drive me to physical therapy thrice a week. I had little strength and great fatigue, and doing household chores, including cooking, was too much for me.

One of my colleagues set up a Meal Train, and I was blessed with great meals two or three days per week for the summer and then later during chemo. Some folks would stay and chat with me for a few minutes, and I realized that I needed these casual conversations because they reminded me of my desire for relationships and my goal of returning to my job at some point.

Many of my friends were constant in my life during the year between my first hospital stay and my transplant, getting groceries for me, picking up prescriptions, cleaning my house, planting and weeding my flower area, etc. I received cards, notes, flower and plant arrangements, emails, and texts regularly. Even though I did not respond to everyone who reached out, I was and am incredibly grateful and humbled by the kindness of others.

Three special friends went even further, one brought me lattes two or three times per month, and I could actually enjoy coffee this way. She occasionally brought me Zoup! soup and just talked with me, not like I was a sick person but as my friend. One of the stories she recounted on one of these visits was a tenet she and her husband had utilized while raising their three children (now adults). "I/We can do hard things." As you have probably realized, this meant a lot to me as I kept that in my mind as I entered into the harvest, transplant, recuperation, and the writing of this story.

Another good friend did household tasks for me; I kept a list of things I could not physically do, and she would come regularly and take care of my *honey-do list*. We would chat while she worked, and again I felt like a human, not a sick person. Third, a longtime childhood friend repeatedly sent cards and texts with words of encouragement and love. Hearing from her was a blessing that always raised my spirits.

Finally, my sister-in-law, Donna, stayed with me the entire month following my transplant; she was an angel. There were so many ways that she helped me, from cooking my meals, cleaning my house, shaving my head, and soothing me when tears overwhelmed me. I am unsure how I would have done it independently in those first few weeks if she had not been with me.

Having these prayer warriors and loving friends in my life was a God thing. I know He had placed these people in my life years prior so they would be here for me now, in my time of greatest need.

CHAPTER 18

Family Is Love

*Love is patient, love is kind. It does not envy, it does not boast,
it is not proud. It is not rude, it is not self-seeking, it is not easily
angered, it keeps no record of wrongs. Love does not delight
in evil but rejoices with the truth. It always protects, always
trusts, always hopes, always perseveres. Love never fails.*
—1 Corinthians 13:4–8

In an earlier chapter, I shared how my children and grandchildren walked me through this entire journey. And though I mentioned my parents and brothers, they supported me through chemo, transplant, and recovery.

Once I was diagnosed and began chemo, my dad accompanied me to seventeen of the twenty sessions. This meant he had to drive thirty minutes to pick me up, sit with me during the treatment, run errands, or get lunch together, and then he had to drive back home.

He also attended doctor appointments with me, the blood marrow transplant team, my nephrologist, my cardiologist, my endocrinologist, and my hematologist. He came to the hospital every day when I was hospitalized for the transplant. I cannot express how meaningful this was to me and how his sacrifice could not be measured. I cherished our conversations on Wednesdays and was reminded how much I value the opinion and insights of my dad. My mom is in poor health and is housebound, so we talked by phone, and I traveled to their home as often as I could.

My brother Dennis and his wife Jamie regularly brought me groceries, sat and visited with me, called me every weekend, walked my dog and clipped her toenails, and did whatever else I needed, and they expected nothing in return. They were selfless and loving; these experiences have brought us closer together as a family.

My brother Joel regularly sent me texts with verses, song lyrics, and stories of encouragement and love. He called me frequently to check in and ask what to pray for. My brother Chuck lives overseas but was back in the States before my stem cell harvest. He took me to a doctor's appointment and talked with me about mundane things and funny stories from our childhood, which made me feel loved and not sick.

Given that my chemo occurred when the COVID vaccine had not been approved for children, I was limited to seeing my grandchildren via FaceTime and occasional visits when everyone was healthy and had tested negative for COVID.

My family gave selflessly, with genuine love and Christian goodwill. I will forever be grateful to God for blessing me with this family.

CHAPTER 19

Recovery and Planning

*My soul finds rest in God alone; my salvation comes
from him. He alone is my rock and my salvation.
He is my fortress. I will never be shaken.*
—Psalms 62:1–2

In October of 2022, I hit my six-month posttransplant day. I began getting my childhood vaccines, along with COVID, influenza, and pneumonia. I also needed to see all my specialist doctors. I needed to get approval from each to go back to work.

Everything looked great; my blood counts were good, and my thyroid-stimulating hormone was in normal ranges for the first time in five years. My triglycerides were coming down and my energy increased daily. I would need to continue to wear my mask in crowded spaces and should avoid large crowds like concerts and sporting events, but the quarantine was over!

I began planning to return to work in January of 2023. I spoke with my department chairperson and began to consult with some of my colleagues on projects that would continue into the spring semester. I began planning for classes and working collaboratively with a new faculty member. And, I felt amazing.

I started meeting friends at coffee shops, doing some of my own grocery shopping, and arranging to attend family gatherings. I planned to have my children and grandchildren at my home during the week after Christmas, and I eagerly planned the menu, looking for new recipes and gathering all the ingredients. I used to love doing these things, but I had not had enough energy for the last few years to do this.

I received permission to travel internationally, began planning for a Liverpool trip in June 2023, and worked with two colleagues to recruit students and make plans for the trip.

I received boosters of many of my vaccines in December and will continue getting new boosters throughout the next eighteen months.

It is the weekend before the start of the spring of 2023 semester, and I am ready! My classes are planned, our online management system is completed, and I have contacted my students to welcome them to my class. After not completing a semester since the fall of 2020 (and that in hybrid form), I am ready to resume my regular duties as a professor of education!

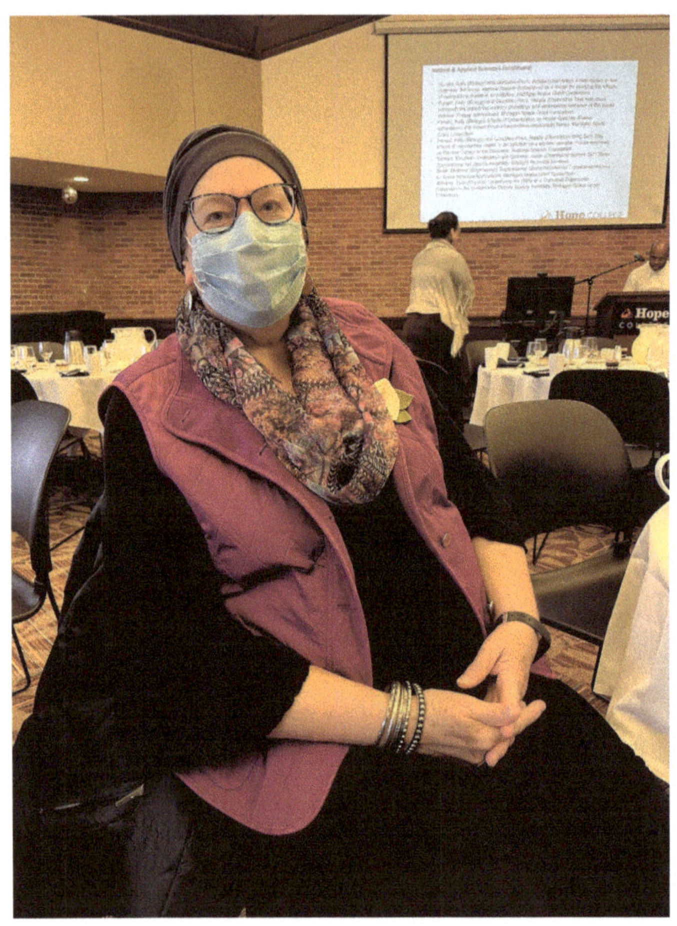

Laura's first day back to school in January 2023 at a faculty luncheon

CHAPTER 20

I Can Do Hard Things

Darkness cannot drive out darkness; only light can do that.
Hate cannot drive out hate; only love can do that.
—Martin Luther King Jr.

If you have faith as a small as a mustard seed, you can
say to this mountain, move from here to there and it
will move. Nothing will be impossible for you.
—Matthew 17:20–21

In hindsight, as I reflected on the last five years of my health journey, I realized that I never asked about my life expectancy once I had been diagnosed. Amyloidosis is a rare blood disorder, and effective treatments had only recently been realized. In fact, when I told my parents what my potential diagnosis was (after meeting with Dr. S in August 2021), my mom googled the disease. She found several articles that mentioned a two-to-five-year life expectancy from diagnosis.

However, the more information I gleaned from Dr. S, the doctors at Mayo, and later the BMT team, the clearer the picture became. Because the disease is hard to diagnose even now, one can imagine how difficult it was to diagnose it thirty to forty years ago. So in most cases of quick death following an amyloidosis diagnosis, it was because the disease had progressed to a point where it was hard to treat successfully.

Additionally, an effective chemo treatment also took a while to perfect, even to the point where the fourth drug added to my chemo cocktail, Darzalex, was a recent addition, and research studies were emerging showing its positive effect on eradicating amyloids.

There are three stages of amyloidosis. When I was finally diagnosed, I was in stage 2; even with a strong medical team, many specialists, and several years, it took a long time to find the diagnosis. In fact, when I shared with my primary doctor what my diagnosis was, she had to read/learn about it as it was something she had not heard about.

I never considered not pursuing treatment or giving up. I never imagined that I would die from whatever plagued me for so long. I simply plodded along and did my best at each phase of the process. And I remained faithful, coveting prayers, asking for God's grace and mercy, and never giving up. Many people have mentioned to me along the journey that I was so strong, that I was brave, and that I maintained a positive attitude.

I never thought of myself as being brave; I simply woke up each day and did what I needed to do. I admit there were times when I felt sorry for myself and when I lamented why this had happened to me, but I never gave into a dark place. (I had experienced other adversity in my life, and through those incidents, I think I had learned that endless worrying was not helpful, and I just needed to be calm and carry on.)

I never considered myself exceptionally positive; at times, the entire journey felt surreal, like it was happening to someone else. I knew it was happening, but it wasn't involving me daily.

What strengthened me was my faith in a loving God whom I knew would not desert me and who hold me up in times of struggle. I read somewhere that while God might give us more than we can handle, He will never give us more than He can handle. I have felt this multiple times in my life, and this knowledge both comforts and sustains me.

The mantra "I can do hard things" and the verse in Philippians, "I can do everything through him who gives me strength" guided my reactions and interactions throughout my health journey. I remain grateful, humbled, and immersed in the mercy of our loving God.

Laura and her grandchildren in July 2023 fourteen months posttransplant

ABOUT THE AUTHOR

Laura Pardo is a mother, a daughter, a grandmother, a sister, a friend, and a child of God. Like most Christians, she often fails in her endeavors to live for Christ, but through God's grace, she rises, as the story of her health journey demonstrates. Pardo spends her spare time writing and conducting grandma camps with her six grandchildren each summer. She has written professional articles and chapters in edited books focusing on teacher education. She has also written a series of books for her grandchildren, depicting her childhood memories. She is a lifelong learner and educator. She has taught elementary, middle, high school, and undergraduates for over forty years. She is currently a teacher educator and educational researcher at a small Christian college.